GOD HAS NOT FORGOTTEN YOU

FUNMILOLA OLUNIFESI

DEDICATION

To all ladies who are waiting for their spouses.

"A worthwhile book for both singles and married people."
- Dr. (Mrs.) Dorcas Bawo, Educationist and Marriage Counsellor

"God has not forgotten you is a must read for every single woman who wants to know God's will for her marriage. Through her wealth of experience as a marriage counsellor, Funmilola answers the core questions that come to mind when thinking about marriage."
– Mrs. Dooshima Ivue, Marriage Counsellor

How can a youth live a good life? By studying and living out God's word, listening to the holy spirit and learning from the experiences of fellow believers. This book gives youths insights on God's word and plan for their married lives.
- Mr. Laolu Thomas, Youth Counsellor

CONTENTS

ACKNOWLEDGMENTS

I give great thanks to: The Almighty God, for the inspiration given me to write this book.

My gratitude also goes to my loving husband, Pastor Lawrence Oluwakayode Olunifesi, for your priceless advice, prayers, moral and financial support.

Thanks to Eunice, Emmanuel and Joseph for your brilliant contributions. The Lord will honour and bless you all.

I do appreciate my friends in the Lord: Mrs. Dupe Oni, Dr. (Mrs.) Dorcas Bawo, Mrs. Mfon Essien, Mrs. Jumoke Mekiliuwa, Mrs. Peju Adekanye, Mrs. Lola Aribido and Mrs. Dooshima Ivue.

Thanks to Mr. and Mrs. Laolu Thomas for your prayers and valuable contributions to the success of this work.

My gratitude also goes to Mr. and Mrs. Ropo Okeya, for your prayers and sacrificial lives of giving. May God bless you and perfect all that concerns you, in Jesus' name.

PROLOGUE

Several years ago, a child was born into the family of Mr. and Mrs. Jones who lived in Lagos. The child's naming ceremony drew men and women of timber and caliber. As it is with the birth of any child, prayers were offered gleefully. She was given the principles of life and godly teachings like the biblical Timothy whose grand mother, Lois and mother Eunice, taught the unfeigned faith, as affirmed by Apostle Paul.

Shirley Jones was taken through the rudiments of the Holy Book. Her primary and secondary education were without a hitch and, within the twinkle of an eye, she adventured into the tertiary institution, where the real school of life began.

Shirley and Sammy hailed from different parts of the country and were older than each other with few years. Sammy's father, Mr. Oreoluwa was a business magnate, while his mother was a nurse. Like most parents, Sammy's father had the best plan for his only child but that dream was not to be realized as death cut his life short in his prime. The task of raising the little boy was left for his mother and niece, Jay. Despite all odds, Sammy grew up to become a responsible man. His mother became a born again Christian three years after the death of her husband and she imparted godly traits into the life of her only son.

God, the perfect matchmaker, had the plan of bringing these two hearts together but it was not to be on a platter of gold, especially because human beings, being what we are, would not want to do God's bidding naturally and this, coupled with the forces of life, may derail the fulfillment of dreams.

These traits were replicated in the lives of Shirley and Sammy; they were meant for each other but the events of life rocked the boats of their lives like a baby whose mother is pacifying to sleep. Their dreams were fading off gradually but destiny and the will of God must be fulfilled in the lives of his children. After a long while, they came together and all they could do to appreciate God's mercy and love was to sing the old glorious tune. "Blessed assurance, Jesus is mine", as they walked joyfully down the aisles.

ONE

MY WEDDING

Blessed assurance, Jesus is mine!
Oh! What a foretaste of glory divine!
Heir of salvation, purchase of God,
Born of His Spirit, washed in His blood.

> Chorus: This is my story, this is my song,
> Praising my Saviour all the day long,
> This is my story; this is my song,
> Praising my Saviour all the day long.

Perfect submission, perfect delight,
Visions of rapture now burst on my sight,
Angels descending, bring from above,
Echoes of mercy, whispers of love.

Perfect submission, all is at rest,
I in my Saviour am happy and blest,
Watching and waiting, looking above,
Filled with His goodness, lost in His love.

The glory of God filled the air as Shirley and Sammy sang this song holding each other cheerfully; their hearts filled with thanksgiving to their Maker as they beamed with smile while they walked into the church for their wedding. Shirley had looked forward to this glorious day as she attained adulthood, having graduated as a Medical Doctor at the age of twenty-eight. Her parents had been expectant that within a short time, their first daughter would be betrothed to a man of her choice.

Born thirty-nine years ago into a family of three: a boy and two girls. Shirley's parents are educated; hence, they saw the need to invest in the education of their children. As God-fearing parents, their kids were well presented before God at a very tender age; Shirley, Paul and Grace, the youngest of the children were taught to uphold Christian virtues. No wonder, Shirley sailed through her primary and secondary education excellently. She scored good grades in all her papers in the

West African School Certificate Examination (WASCE) and also in the Joint Admissions and Matriculation Board (JAMB) Examination. Hence, she had no problem securing admission into the premier university in the South –West geo-political zone of Nigeria to study Medicine.

While still in the secondary school, she had love proposition from some male classmates but such advances were bluntly refused as she was known to be of good behavior; keeping herself chaste before matrimony was a cardinal value she had been taught.

Preparations towards this glorious day started in earnest. The couple, having being cleared by the Marriage Committee of Shirley's church and with a letter of recommendation from her spouse's church attesting to his active membership of the assembly as a "worker "in the Ushering Department. Shirley had been a conscientious worker in the Children's /Teenagers' section of her church. Their plans were committed to God in prayer by inviting His presence and asking for His peace, provision and protection before, during and after the wedding. As they walked radiantly into the church, their gaze fixed on each other, they were overwhelmed with joy for the inception of a new life.

The wedding ceremony lasted one-and-a-half hours with a message from the officiating priest admonishing them to stick to Jesus Christ who is able to see them through their marriage. According to him, the wedding ceremony "is just a shadow of things to come", urging that love, sincerity and closeness to God should be the bedrock of their home. The parents, relations, friends and well-wishers were also advised to keep off the new home and allow the new couple to build their home together.

For the bride, Shirley, the man of God advised her to accept that she had been joined in holy matrimony with a peculiar person from a different background and a special upbringing and so should love and submit to him. Sammy, on the other hand, was told to be tolerant with his wife and bear her in love, especially considering the circumstances of his upbringing. His mother, as a single parent brought him up, since he lost his father at a very tender age. All he could boast of about an ideal home was what his auntie, Jay and his mother taught him: lessons about life, food preparation and mode of dressing: as well as the word of God.

After the pastor's message, it was time to sign the dotted lines on the Marriage Register. The parents of the new couple and two representatives from each family went into the vestry while the rest of the congregation sang and danced cheerfully. The couple used the "signet ring" of their signatures to seal the union.

The wedding service ended with the recessional hymn, **"O God our Help in Ages Past"**. As the bridal train walked through the aisles, they were cheered on by the ecstatic throng of family members, friends and well-wishers. It was indeed a glorious day for the new couple, their parents and everybody at the occasion.

The new couple, still basking in the euphoria of the wedding proceeded to the city of Jos, in the northern geo-political zone of Nigeria for their honeymoon. Four days into the honeymoon, they decided to visit a major market in town for sightseeing and shopping. It was at this place that Shirley stumbled on her old friend. Debby, who hailed from Pankshin in Plateau State. "Shirley, Shirley", shouted Debby. Shirley looked back and, noticing her friend, ran towards her and both of them were caught in a warm hug.

Sammy stood in amazement, wondering who on earth this friend could be that is wife left him with such speed. Debby was also stunned seeing her ally in the same attire with a young handsome man. Although, Sammy was a bit older than his wife, age is a matter of the heart. You are what you say your age is. In other words, the inward and outward presentation of a person is what the age is. After all, "Life", they say, "begins at forty".

"Shirley, is this your husband?" asked Debby excitedly.

"Yes, oh! Meet Sammy Oreoluwa," answered Shirley with a feeling of fulfillment.

Sammy gave her a warm handshake and they exchanged pleasantries.

"I hope you're enjoying the serene weather of Jos and the tourist attractions," enthused Debby.

"It is a wonderful place to be," Sammy replied curtly.

Debby excused her friend from her spouse and exclaimed in amazement.

"Shirley, God has finally answered your prayers after all the painful and bitter experiences that you went through", remarked Debby, obviously envious of her friend's new found love.

"Sometimes you have to walk on rough pathways to become stronger and reliable. If I tell you my adventure on the marital journey and what it turned out to be, you would be shocked, but I give God all the glory," answered

Shirley.

"We will be having a Single Sisters' Forum in our church on Saturday and I will be glad if you can come and share some of your testimonies with them to strengthen their faith, so that they can know that God is faithful to all those who trust in Him, " said Debby.

"Can you tell my husband" demanded Shirley.

"Why not, I'll do that right away", uttered Debby, encouraged by her friend's response.

Debby walked up to Sammy to seek his consent for his heartthrob to share her experience with the unmarried ladies in the church. Debby is a born again Christian and the coordinator of the Sisters' fellowship of a vibrant Pentecostal church located in the heart of Jos. After her departure, the love-struck couple continued their 'sight-seeing' and on getting back to the hotel where they lodged, they set apart a day to seek God's face in prayer and fasting for the programme.

TWO

MY TESTIMONY

At the scheduled time of 2.p.m…, the seminar started with an opening prayer and was followed by a worship and praise session to the Most High. Since God inhabits the praises of His people, all the living souls must come to Him with a heart full of thanksgiving, irrespective of their conditions. This was why the hall was filled to capacity with people who appreciate the goodness, mercy, unfailing love and faithfulness of God.

At the end of the praise and worship session, the congregation was led into a prayer session, after which the seminar began. Debby introduced Shirley and her husband shortly before the former made straight for the podium to deliver the message of hope to the expectant youths. But before doing this, she led them into another session of worship in songs. Prayers were thereafter offered to consecrate the people and asked the Holy Spirit to take charge of the entire meeting.

"I want to thank God for the opportunity given to me to give this testimony. At a particular point in my life, what I went through were trials, challenges and tests of my faith;

but because God is alive, all these trials and temptations have become testimonies. This will be your too, in Jesus' name. I gave my life to Christ at the age of seventeen, shortly after my secondary education. The following year, I gained admission into the university to study medicine".

"While in the university, I got engaged to a "brother" called Jide, a law student in the same institution. He was a zealous child of God, who was convinced of the relationship as much as I was. Ours was not the case of love at first sight; we prayed individually, were led to each other and the love grew thereafter. Few members of the executive, including the president, were aware of our relationship. During the courtship, we engaged each other in a lot of activities like prayers, Bible Study and occasional visits, since we were both serious students".

"The relationship continues for two years, and I really looked forward to the day both of us would be joined in holy matrimony and start a family. I believe this is the dream of every lady seated in this hall. The audience shouted a thundering "Amen".

"In the course of our courtship, I noticed something dubious about Jide; his correspondence was always hidden from me. This did not really disturb me because I trusted him and did not want to bother about his private life. But I was proved wrong. On one occasion, I was in his room when one of his classmates came to inform him that he had a visitor in the common room. I wanted to go with him but as usual, he objected. When he came back fifteen minutes later, he told me on inquiry that the visitor was a friend whom his mother sent to him with some food stuff.

"On another occasion, he was out of the campus when one of his friends gave me a letter sent from his town. Since I was forbidden from reading his mails, I gave it to him as soon as he returned. Unknown to me, I had become the laughing stock outside our fellowship, since none of our members would ever imagine that "Brother Jide" a house fellowship and unit leader was "double-dealing".

"The Bible says, **"Even members of your own family will be your enemies". (Matthew 10:36).**

Six months into the third year of our courtship, the cat was let out of the bag: Jide had collected a Christian novel from me and, while returning it, had forgotten a letter written by another lady inside. Dammy, the writer, was based in Lagos and had been the unknown guest visiting and writing letters to him. I read through the letter, completely stunned. It read:

My Dear Jide,
It's quite an age! I got your letter, thanks very much. I am doing fine by the grace of God and my job is going very well. Did you receive the money I sent to you the other day? I am yet to receive this month's salary, but as soon as we are paid, I will send more money to you as requested.

I'm all yours,
Dammy

I became depressed by this development, but was instructed and comforted by God's word of peace in

Philippians 4::7: And because you belong to Christ Jesus, God's peace will stand guard over all your thoughts and feelings. His peace can do this far better than our human minds.

"I went with the letter demanding an explanation. He was shocked to the bones. "Is this why you never allow me to read your letters? I didn't know you have skeletons in your cupboard. Jide, you are a heartless being. What have I done to deserve this shabby treatment? I shouted in anger.

"It's not what you think, God is my witness; I was only dating Dammy to pave my way through school. You are the one I love; I need her to sponsor some minor expenses since my parents are incapable of meeting all my needs", explained Jide. He had hardly finished when I snapped at him furiously, "And you think the best thing to do is to use an innocent girl for your selfish desire and dump either of us at the end of your course? No wonder the Bible says; "The heart of man is desperately wicked, who can know it?" Then you have the guts to use God as your witness. God is not an author of confusion and He cannot be a friend to a liar like you. I have been too simple and naïve to believe you, thanks so much, Jide.

"I left in annoyance to see the president of the Christian fellowship and presented the letter to him. Jide was called to explain and it was then I discovered that his parents were aware of his relationship with Dammy and they had given their consent. But as he said, he was only trying to see if his foul play would enable him use the girl's money, only to be dumped thereafter for a more suitable partner like me. The fact that Dammy had only a School Certificate was an issue I did not bother myself with. I then resolved that going ahead with this kind of man would amount to building a home on a sandy foundation. That was why how I dropped everything about Jide.

"Perhaps, you may want to ask, "Didn't both of you pray and were convinced that it was God who led you to each other"? Yes, we prayed, but the problem is not with God but man.

THREE

RETREAT FROM MEN

After my ordeal with Jide, I decided to go into what I called "A Retreat from Men", and it was executed successfully for two years. All advances from men were out rightly rebuffed. When I was in my fifth year, I told God I was ready for another relationship and pleaded for mercy because I knew I had blocked my ears to His injunctions all the while. I did not bother to pray at all whenever friendship propositions came from men, whether they were believers or not; I bluntly refused.

I remember a brother who said God told him that I was his future partner; in a brief moment, I dismissed his advance by saying that even if God told me he was my spouse, I would not pay heed to his instruction. Ironically, he did not give up until he realized I meant every bit of what I said. He later changed his prayers and God led him to another lady who accepted his offer of love.

"Obviously, God will speak to man, but it is left to man

to accept His wish; hence, it is necessary to seek God's face for His will in every aspect of our lives and also ask for the grace to do His will. This is because God will not force us to follow His commandments; the willingness must come from us.

"How often has the Lord spoken to you and you have bluffed Him by rejecting His directions? With my readiness to do His will in my fifth year, I fell prey to a man who I thought was a Christian because of lack of patience and my desire for affluence. Since my relationship with a young undergraduate was a failure, I felt a mature man would be a more reasonable and responsible person with the fear of God.

God is not moved by our feelings, but only by His words, through different mediums of reaching out to us and our own means of getting to His throne of grace. These are through worship, praises, Bible Study and unhindered service that must be rendered with a pure heart. In the book of Isaiah 55:8-9, the Bible says:

The Lord says, 'My thoughts are not like yours. Your ways are not like mine. Just as the heavens are higher than the earth, so my ways are higher than your ways, and my thoughts are higher than thoughts.

Men are prone to be rash and quick in their judgments, but God is ever faithful and consistent. You may be wrong to use the outward appearance of someone or who he associates with to describe how religious or close to God the person should be. We were in the lecture room one day when a student from another department beckoned on me while I was having a serious discussion on an assignment given to us by one of my lecturers. "Shirley, Mr. Raymond would like to see you in his office", cut in the student.

Mr. Raymond is a Christian who was highly respected among the students because of his high morals and

Christian standards. While many lecturers would want to have carnal knowledge of a female student as a condition for getting good grades in the examination, he stuck to Christian principles; indeed, he was an angel to the student community.

"With all his good credentials; I never thought this lecturer could keep the company of a colleague who was merely a nominal Christian. I would describe him as such because his father was a reverend in a protestant church and his mother a virtuous woman. Having been raised in a Christian home, he thought this was all he needed to be a Christian. He seemed oblivious of the fact that we are only saved by grace and faith in God, salvation is God's gift to us; it is not anything we acquire on how own or something we earn or inherit.

"Teddy, as fondly called by all his admirers and associates, was a noticeable figure at the gathering of the saints, especially at the meetings of the elite. He featured prominently at seminars, breakfast meetings, and other occasions organized to reach out to the crème-de-la-crème of the society. With his closeness to genuine Christians, he could easily dissemble and this was why I easily fell to his love proposal.

He was in his thirties, a banker by profession and by sheer coincidence; we are from the same tribe. But it did not occur to me then that all these factors do not really count when deciding whom you will spend the rest of your life with. But that rather, what one should look out for is the mind of God for one's life, not what is considered right or wrong. In short, intending couples must ensure that they are compatible in faith".

"I had no peace within me and the president of our fellowship warned that I should not accept his proposal. Beloved sisters, I was anxious to be engaged; although I was still an undergraduate. I felt time was not on my side and that I was getting older by the day.

Each morning, when I stood before the mirror and

looked at myself; the devil would tell me, "Shirley, you are not getting younger, and if you ignore Teddy, you have missed everything and it will be difficult to get another man. Take a look at him; he is handsome, averagely rich, educated, loving and God-fearing. Why don't you accept his proposal?" Another voice would whisper gently into my ear,

"Wait on the Lord's help. Be strong and brave, and wait for the Lord's help. Weeping may endure for a night, but joy comes in the morning". (Psalms 27:14; 30:5b)

At this point, I would become annoyed and mutter to myself, "For how long will I wait; a responsible person has come my way now and all I hear is wait, be courageous. God, can't you understand?" My heart was filled with anxiety and love for mundane things and I failed to be instructed in the Word of God which says:

So, I tell you, don't worry about the things you need to live – what you will eat, drink, or wear. Life is more important than food, and the body is more important than what you put on it. Look at the birds. They don't plant, harvest, or save food in barns, but your heavenly Father feeds them. Don't you know you are worth much more than they are? (Matthew 6:25-26)

"Most of us are guilty of anxiety and when we put up this act, we make God a liar and present Him as if He has forgotten us. He has a plan and a purpose for your life; He has the schedule of your life in His throne room. The fact that "Laura" got married immediately after graduating from school or even while still in school does not mean it must be the same way with you. God's plan for Sister Abimbola's life may be different from yours and you know quite well that no two children from the same parents are the same.

The plan and purpose of God for Joseph, the dreamer, and his brethren were different. Queen Esther was an orphan, but when the time came for her to be celebrated, she was brought into limelight through destiny. I prophesy into your life that you will manifest at the appointed time, in Jesus' name.

"In the midst of all these, I decided to do it my own way by getting engaged to Teddy and put God to test, a high magnitude of sin. I kept it from the president of my fellowship for a while and accepted Teddy's proposal with a conclusion that I would use it to verify if he was a good Christian or not. Remember, I had heard from God that this case was a closed matter, an outright disobedience to God.

It is better to obey the Lord than to offer sacrifices to him. It is better to listen to him than offer the fat from rams.

(I Samuel 15:22b).

FOUR

HOT COAL

I started dating Teddy secretly, warning him not to visit me in the school or send his friend to me. I agreed to do all the "visiting", and that, at irregular intervals, I would go to the market to buy some foodstuff and prepare food for him for the weekend. Unlike Jide, I could not vouch for Teddy's moral behavior. But I was too much enamored of him to notice that each time I visited that he would talk about neither prayers nor Bible Study. I was at fault because I used to visit him alone in his flat at the Government Reservation Area (G.R.A). He would always say, "Haven't you had enough of prayers and Bible Study? Let's discuss something else.

"How did I ever think I could put a hot coal on my bosom and it would not burn my cloth? I arrogated God's responsibility to myself. In replying his words, I would say, "The devil gives an idle hand something to do; let's invite the Holy Spirit into this union" He would agree reluctantly at times and, on other occasions, he would decline. I was forced to move in his direction as he would prefer that we preoccupy ourselves with playing ludo, chess, monopoly and the likes. Within a short time, he advanced from ludo game to proposing sex, which I bluntly refused to oblige, since it was contrary to my belief in purity before marriage. It was not too long before I got into serious trouble with Teddy. I had thought that I would be able to influence Teddy into giving his life to Christ. Beloved sisters, I got it all wrong; no man's salvation is in our hands, but it is the Holy Spirit who does the work.

My son, remember my words. Don't forget what I have told you. Consider my teaching as precious as your own eyes. Obey my commands, and you will have a good life. Tie them around your finger. Write them on your heart. Treat wisdom like the woman you love and knowledge like the one dearest to you. Wisdom will save you from that other woman, the other man's wife, who tempts you with such sweet words. (Proverb 7:1-5)

"On this fateful day, I had made up my mind that this was going to be my last visit to him at home. When I got there, I knocked on the door as usual and he came out to open it for me and went back immediately. Then he came back a few minutes later and we exchanged pleasantries. You look gloomy today, is there any problem? asked Teddy, as he drew closer to me on the chair. "Oh! No qualms, I'm fine", I replied. Can I have a word with you in the room? He asked again. "This place will be better, I'm all ears", I replied.

"Before I could say any other thing, he had dragged me into the bedroom and made a move to unbutton my blouse. Prior to this action, while helping me to take care of what I brought into the kitchen, I noticed that he had locked the main door leading to the house but I thought he did that for security reasons. The whole episode was no longer funny to me. "Why did you lock the door and kept the ley in your pocket?' I inquired. "Nothing much", he responded jokingly.

"A lot of things went on in my mind as I started

pleading for mercy within me, because I knew it was only God that would rescue me from the impending danger that I willingly led myself into. "Have mercy on me Oh! Lord", I muttered to myself quietly. I knelt down before Teddy, pleading that he should desist from his devilish move."

"Haven't I tried Shirley? You've been tempting me all this while; I can no longer stand this burning desire within me towards you everyday. I'm also pleading that you should let me do it just this once", he said furtively in his desperation.

"Do you know what this once can lead to? It will ruin my life and career. It could result into an unwanted pregnancy from pre-marital sex and lifetime guilt", I importuned.

"Teddy was not in any way moved by my plea. I tried to run away, but there was no way; he rushed towards me again like an angry and hungry lion that has just caught its prey for the day. In a bid to free myself from his grip, I laid my hand on a piece of iron rod lying on the floor of the room and hit him on the head. Blood ran freely from his head and he cried with pain. Fear gripped me and I started crying too. Then, it occurred to me that I had not taken enough precautionary measures before going into the relationship.

You are not the same as those who don't believe. So, don't join yourselves to them. Good and evil don't belong together. Light and darkness cannot share the same room.

So, come away from those people and separate yourselves from them, says the Lord. Don't touch anything that is not clean, and I will accept you. I will be your father and you will be my sons and daughter, says the Lord All-Powerful. (II Corinthians 6:14, 17-18).

"As a medical student, I applied the little knowledge of first aid treatment that I know, and we set out instantly for the hospital in a taxi cab. He was on admission for three days. The news of the incident spread like wild fire on the campus. So, to clear myself, I went to Mr. Raymond to narrate my own version of the story flying around. I also declared to him that I was no longer interested in the relationship.

Teddy accepted the break-up, but not until he had reported the matter to the police and I was arrested and detained for two days. Thereafter, I was granted bail and told to report daily at the police station. But for divine intervention, I would have been charged to court and prosecuted for attempted murder.

FIVE

HE FOUND ME

'I went back to the president of my fellowship like the prodigal child and narrated my ordeal. "You need to see a counselor and a deliverance minister, Sister Shirley", he screamed at me. If you know anyone, I don't mind, I am tired of my life", was all I could say to the suggestion in my utter perplexity and helplessness.

During the next holiday, we arranged to see a deliverance minister who took me through a prayer of repentance to obtain mercy from God for my sin of disobedience against God's injunctions. After that, I was taken through a prayer of deliverance from self-guilt and the wiles of the devil were totally destroyed from my life.

"I decided thereafter to live a life of absolute holiness and total submission to his will and commandments; I surrendered my life anew and became more dedicated to the things of God. At the end of my course, I was posted to Lagos State for my National Youth Service Corps. I also did my internship with the Lagos State University Teaching Hospital. By this time, my parents had started getting worried because I was not having a steady relationship. But God's words of hope were my comfort. Whenever my mum pestered me with questions, I would say, I know that **God has not forgotten me**, I am engrafted in the hollow of His hands; His thoughts towards me are thoughts of good and not of evil and He would give me an expected end. "My mum would then beam with smile and nod in agreement with my spirit of optimism.

"Meanwhile, my younger brother, Paul had started making preparations towards his own wedding. Paul's wedding ceremony eventually took place shortly after my NYSC placement. I got a job at the State Hospital as a Trainee Medical Doctor. I started attending a Pentecostal church in the city of Lagos; having been baptized by immersion while in the school.

I was trained as a "worker" in the church and at the end of the training; I was posted to the Children /Teenagers' department of the church. This decision proved beneficial to me and I will advise you to always keep yourself busy on the things of God whether you are waiting on Him for a particular thing or not. As you do that, He will arise on your behalf one day. Remember, your period of waiting will be accounted for. I know a lot of you are in haste; some of you are already thirty years old or above thirty and, in some cases, even over forty, and you think God has forgotten you. Listen to the word of God for you:

But now Zion says, "The Lord has left me; the Lord has forgotten me. But the Lord says, can a woman forget her baby? Can she forget the child who came from her body? Even if she can forget her children, I cannot forget you. I drew a picture of you on my hand, I cannot forget you. (Isaiah 49:14-16)

"I kept praying and trusting Him that his words would be fulfilled in my life one day. I do not pray that the answer to your prayer should linger as long as mine. However, no matter how long or short it may be, ensure your heart is in tune with your Maker. His coming can be at any time and your time can be up at any time too; so, you're not being married will not be an excuse for your inability to make heaven.

"Twelve years after my internship, the reply to my desperate petition to God came; by this time, I had risen to a higher position in my workplace. I have a car and I have built my own house. I also moved my parents from their old house into a befitting three-bedroom bungalow which I built for them I did not allow all these achievements to get into my head and do you know I was still a virgin. Despite all these attainments, I felt a vital part of me was missing and that was a suitable life partner.

"I met my husband for the first time when he came to see my Medical Director. I was on morning duty and the Director had not come into the hospital on this great day. The Medical Consultant brought his case file to my table and I attended to him as instructed by my immediate boss. He was placed on a three-day treatment. Then, he walked up to me on the last day of his treatment to inquire about the church I am attending, I replied innocently.

Two weeks later, my pastor informed me that a certain man came to see him about me. I could not recall the image of the man I had met recently. Within the years of my waiting on the Lord, especially after rededicating my life to Him, I came across a lot of men, Christians and non-Christians; even married men tried to make me give in to their advances, but God was on my side. It was indeed a wearisome period.

"The nature of my job exposes me to a lot of people; men, women and children. A particular wealthy man offered to send me to the United States of America to seek greener pasture in my career. He offered to foot the whole bill for the trip including accommodation and living expenses. A very tempting offer it was, behold, he was married and was not even a Christian. Apparently, working in the United States of America would put me on a much better salary as a Medical Practitioner compared to my present salary, but I remembered that all that glitters is not gold.

Trust in the Lord and wait quietly for his help. Don't be angry when people make evil plans and succeed. (Psalm 37:7)

"The fact that a brother is in the same fellowship or church with you does not guarantee he would be your husband; you must seek God's face to know his plan for your life through prayers. Your conviction; that is, what God wants you to do in marriage and in any other adventure of life will give you the peace of mind and the assurance that he will see you through the trauma that you may likely come across as you continue in life.

The marriage institution is a spiritual project that must be pursued with all seriousness; hence, your conviction is the confidence you have that is God who has led or spoken to you to accept "Brother P's" marriage proposal. It is that assurance that will stir you up to plead your case before God when there are storms in the marriage. If you get married to "Bright" out of steep infatuation or love at first sight, compassion, church connection or ethnic affinity, you have missed it.

'No matter who the person is, pray very well to receive a "yes" from the Lord before accepting the man's proposal. Even if your pastor says he is convinced about the relationship, you need to receive your own conviction too if you are a true child of God. There is no marriage without its storms. How bold will you be before the Lord if you did what your instinct tells you to do or what the circumstances around you dictate?

"Having told me of this "stranger", my pastor advised me to go and pray and report back to him after two weeks; I did as instructed and in the process, I received a word from the Lord that He works in mysterious way and that he had answered my prayers concerning my spouse many years ago.

We know that in everything God works for the good of those who love him. These are the people God chose, because that was his plan. (Romans 8:28)

"The next day was a Saturday. As soon as I resumed work to take over from the doctor on night duty, this man came in while I was signing the duty register.

"Good morning, doctor", he greeted.

"Good morning sir", how may I help you?" I replied.

"I have an appointment with Doctor Frederick", he answered.

"He hasn't come in at the moment", I explained.

"When is he likely to resume?" He asked again.

"He'll be around any moment from now", I responded.

Doctor Frederick entered into the hospital twenty minutes after the man's arrival and I was assigned to attend to him as Doctor Frederick had to do the routine ward round to see the patients on admission. Immediately he came into his office, I sent his patient to him for further check-up. When he was through with the medical director, the man was directed to the pharmacy to collect his drugs. He came back to thank me and left.

"At the end of the service on Sunday, my pastor called me and asked if the Lord had revealed anything to me. I told him that God said his ways are sometimes incomprehensible and that he had answered my prayers, although I did not know the person yet. I am sure there is somebody asking a question. "Why do you have to take such a risk? What if the person is blind, lame, disabled in any way or infected with an incurable disease?'

Total submission to God enables you to accept His will. Consequently, always ask God for the grace to know His will and to do it. If He is the one who has led you into the relationship, no matter the defect, He will see you through. The pastor also affirmed that he had received a go ahead from the Lord after seeking His face. He inquired if I would like to meet with the person and I replied positively. He gave me an appointment for three that afternoon. This is the hour I've longed for all my life, and could hardly wait for the time to roll in.

"Sammy Oreoluwa walked into the pastor's office exactly three o'clock. I had come earlier but stayed elsewhere as they discussed at length on Sammy's mission to the pastor. I didn't see him when he entered, so, when I came in, my heart jumped. After we exchanged pleasantries, I asked him if he was a member of our church.

He said, "no". The pastor introduced him to me as the man who the Lord spoke to as your spouse-to-be, then, I exclaimed involuntary. Then in amazement, I spoke further, "Are you not Mr. Oreoluwa, the patient I have been attending to at the hospital? How are you feeling now?

"I am fine, thank you", he replied with a feeling of relief. Can you tell us your own story, Mr. Oreoluwa, urged the pastor?

"He brought out a card from his Bible, which incidentally was a photograph I took with my colleagues during my internship twelve years ago. One of the ladies in the photograph was Sammy's cousin, Juliet. She was my friend whom I had lost contact with a long time ago. I was reliably informed by another friend of hers that Juliet's fiancée won the American Visa Lottery and she had since relocated to the United States of America.

"According to Sammy, he was praying for a life partner when Juliet visited him in Lagos and showed him the picture. Looking through the picture, he said the Holy Spirit ministered to him that I was the answer to his prayers. However, he kept the revelation to himself for two days before asking Juliet who I was, but Juliet's explanation did not yield anything positive. I met Juliet during my internship, but we were not close friends. She left for her base without any means of locating me for twelve years. Meanwhile, the relationships Sammy had with ladies subsequently failed woefully.

"As he explained further, he had grown impatient with God wondering how long he would wait for this person whom he did not know. His situation became worse by the fact that ladies in his church tagged him as "possessed brother" because he was falling in and out of relationships. He confirmed that he was tired of waiting and wanted to work things out in his own way.

Three years ago, he said he decided to hand over everything to the Lord by asking God to lead him to where his partner is. What brought him to the hospital was diagnosed as malaria fever after running a test, which was not that severe. Initially, with the symptoms of body weakness and headache, a friend directed him to the hospital, but he declined by saying, "When last did I visit the hospital? All I need is to rest and I'll take some days off", he told his friends.

"After nine days rest at home, his condition worsened and only then did he take to his friend's advice. On his first visit to the hospital, he was attended to by Doctor Frederick. When he called at the clinic again, he met me for the first time and the lord confirmed to him that I was the lady he had been longing to meet all these years. That was why he did not hesitate to ask about my name and my place of worship. When he got home that day, he brought out the picture to confirm that I was the person. He decided not to waste any time again, but went straight to see my pastor.

Beloved, your present predicament will bring out

something good from your life. As busy as he is as an architect, God had to break him down with malaria fever to answer his long-standing prayers.

"What amazed me most is how God allowed the two of us to wander for twelve years before we could meet each other. The twelve years of wandering was not a waste but a time to draw closer to God, a time of renewal of strength and a time to test the depth of our faith in our Creator to do what He has purposed for our lives.

Our coming together in a way we never envisaged as made us to appreciate each other very much. "Indeed, God works in mysterious ways", declared the pastor, who prayed for us and counseled us as follows:

"Having received God's perfect will; let me encourage you with these words to guide you before and whenever you want to start your courtship".

- Pray and wait on the Lord to receive who your spouse is.
- Prayerfully meet your pastor or any trusted Christian elder who is a counselor that you can confide in.
- After you have been prayed with and certified okay to start a relationship, you can proceed to take the next step.
- You should attend the Intending Couples' Counseling Classes in your church.
- You must know that you have been bought with a price that is immeasurable.
- Avoid premarital sex. Keep your body pure to enable God dwell in you to avoid been destroyed.

I Corinthians 6:16-17.

Let the spirit of God dwell in you all the time.

Galatians 5:16, 19.

You must know that once you have agreed to start a relationship with a brother and you are in love with him, he is different from any other man. What goes on in your minds towards each other is a "mystery of love"

Do not exchange books that will arouse your emotions during courtship. For example, books on sex, fertility, pregnancy, and childbirth.

Do not exchange gifts that can also arouse your emotions. For examples, gifts of panties, boxers, brassier, underskirts and all internal wears. Don't go to a brother's home alone.

As a lady, do not expose your body carelessly in the presence of your spouse-to-be and do not sleep in the same room with him before marriage no matter the circumstance or pressure, especially when it is few weeks to your wedding.

Spend time with him judiciously by praying, studying the Bible, and discussing things that will benefit your home in the future.

Tell each other the answers to the following questions: Were you engaged before? Do you have a child already? Have you ever committed an abortion? How many men were you engaged to before the current relationship? Have you ever jilted anyone or were you jilted? What led to the break-up in your previous relationships, if you were in any? The answers to these questions will help you in your present engagement.

Share your bitter and pleasant experiences with him. It will help you to know what to pray for and if you need to go for deliverance.

Tell each other about your family backgrounds. Are you aware of a generational curse or sickness in your family?

Love plays a major role in a relationship of this nature. Both of you must love each other as outlined in I Corinthians 13.

The courtship period is a time to know each other, that is, your likes and dislikes; it is a time to know about your relatives and in-laws.

However, there are things you do not do together during courtship; watch your closeness and try as much as possible not to be together alone.

Don't give in to lustful desires from your prospective spouse in the name of love and do not visit each other in discreet places and at odd hours. For example, a peck on the cheek, a kiss, staring endlessly at each other, a romance, and caressing or touching of sensitive parts of your bodies.

Remember, **I Timothy 4:12 says, "You are young but don't let anyone treat you as if you are not important. Be an example to show the believers how they should live. Show them by what you say, by the way you live, by your love, by your faith, and by your pure life.**

When love grows beyond its limits during courtship, it becomes lust, defilement, and it will make you unworthy before God. So many youths indulge in premarital sex and face the consequences. If only the ways some of these ladies and men lived unchaste lives during the hay days were revealed, they would have saved the people interceding for them from unending cry for mercy and divine intervention.

Most often than not, the predicaments of most couples are the product of their ungodly acts during courtship.

Your different backgrounds will necessitate different approaches to the issues of life. Learn to forgive and forget when you offend each other, because it is bound to happen. Be moderate in all things and do not be a spendthrift.

She further advised the audience to find out about

the counseling for those planning to get married in our churches and enroll immediately.

"This was how I started dating my husband".

Shirley concluded her story, as she planted a passionate kiss on her husband's cheek, beaming with smile. She rounded off with the following words:

Beloved sisters, God has not forgotten you. He has a plan and a purpose for your life. You will reach your goals in life, just wait for him. Do not be in a hurry. Even if you are held bound by the forces of darkness, the God we are serving is a consuming fire and He will release His fire to consume all the works of darkness in your life, in Jesus' name.

"Peradventure, if there is anyone in our midst who has not accepted Jesus Christ into her life, you must have learnt one or two things from my testimony. Life without Christ is a life in crisis. You need someone who will lead, guide and direct you; and there is no other person who can do this except the Lord Jesus Christ.

Do not agree with the devil that it is over with you in marriage. Say "no" to the antics of Satan. Turn around and look at Jesus with His arm stretched towards you and He is saying, "Daughter, do not be afraid, I have not forgotten you. I have a plan for creating you. Why don't you accept my offer of love and salvation? Cast all your burdens upon me because I care for you. My yoke is easy and my burden is light.

It does not matter where you are now or what you have done to yourself, you can pick the bits and pieces of your life and hand it over to God, He will take them from you and do something marvelous with your life. When I handed over my life to Jesus Christ, He turned it around and gave me the best gift that He had prepared for me from the foundation of the world. He can do the same for you, if you will allow him today. We have had a long day; shall we rise up to thank God for this wonderful program".

"An altar was made for those who would love to give their lives to Jesus Christ and those who wanted to rededicate their lives to their Creator. Many members of the audience answered the call. It was indeed a harvest of souls to God's kingdom".

Nine months after wedding, the couple gave birth to a set of beautiful twins: a boy and a girl. Due to the nature of the meeting, questions were asked and answers given. These are taken care of in the next chapter.

SIX

QUESTIONS AND ANSWERS

1. Having waited for so long as a spinster, I have a feeling that God has forgotten me.

First of all, you have to deal with your feelings and thoughts. Make sure your feelings and thoughts are in line with God's promises and desires for your life. God loves you and He wants the best for you, but He also has the right timing to bring His plans to pass in your life. God has spoken, you should believe his words and that settles it. Secondly, He has not forgotten you; he is only preparing and nurturing you for the brighter days.

> **Can a woman forget her baby? Can she forget the child who came from her body? Even if she can forget her children, I cannot forget you. (Isaiah 49:15)**

> **I say this because I know the plans that I have towards you. This message is from the Lord. "I have good plans for you. I don't plan to hurt you. I plan to give you hope and a future.**

(Jeremiah 29:11)

2. I have delved into many sins; I am the architect of my problems, can God forgive me?

"All that God demands from you is a repentant heart that will confess, forsake and continuously live in holiness through the grace and the mercy of God that is available at Calvary. There is an abundant blood flowing to wash away your sins, but do not make sin your hobby.

> **Whoever hides their sins will not be successful, but whoever confesses their sins and stops doing wrong will receive mercy. (Proverbs 28:13)**

> **But if we confess our sins, God will forgive us. He always does what is right. He will make us clean from all the wrong things we have done. (I John 1:9)**

3. How can I know the mind of God concerning my marital life?

God's words are His mind for you; study the Bible and "key" yourself into His words and you will know His mind for you. Additionally, your closeness to God will determine how you will be hearing from him. For instance, He can speak to you through the Bible, prophecy, word of wisdom, word of knowledge, audible voice, vision, revelation, a still small voice, dreams, circumstances, godly counsel and by the way he speaks to you.

As you get closer to the Lord, you will learn to be quiet in your inner man and not be noisy; avoid sin and distractions. You will be able to identify His voice as He speaks through whatever means that He will decide to use to communicate to you. You must prepare your heart to receive from Him by praying, fasting, studying the Bible, listening to Him and by being watchful against manipulations and your desires that may not really be God's plan for you. I must confess that this is a spiritual height and closeness to God that all His children must work assiduously to attain.

Suffice it is to say that your mode of hearing from God may not be the same with another person, but whatever you hear must be checked with the word of God. His words are His mind and ethics or principles for man.

> **Your word is like a lamp that guides my steps, a light that shows the path I should take. (Psalm 119:105)**

> **Lord, your rules are wonderful. That is why I follow them. As people understand your word, it brings light to their lives. Your word makes even simple wise. Your word makes simple people wise. (Psalm 119:129-130)**

4. How mature should a man or woman be before getting married?

Either party must be spiritually and emotionally matured before venturing into marriage, and need not to be a Methuselah or a baby before going into the union. Different denominations and groups have different ages for their members to be married.

Although you may not need to have the whole world prior to your marriage; the man must be financially alright to be able to take care of his new bride and himself. You should also have your own accommodation, no matter how small. It is not wise to get married and take the bride to your parent's home. Your wife may have issues with getting to understand too many people at the initial stage of your marriage and if care is not taken, it may affect the peace and the success of your marriage. Both of you need to leave the physical attachments to your families and cleave to each other because you have a lot to know about each other. This may require some adjustments from both of you and it will be gradual.

The wife must be prepared to assist in making financial contributions to the home as a good "help meet" to her husband. Marriage is meant for mature man and woman and not for teenagers. Spiritual, physical, mental, emotional and financial maturities are all recommended.

> **And God said, that is why a man will leave his father and mother and be joined to his wife. And the two people will become one. (Matthew 19:5)**

> **Everyone should take care of all their own people. Most important, they should take care of their own family. If they do not do that, then do not accept what we believe. They are worse than someone who does not even believe in God. (I Timothy 5:8)**

5. What should I do if God impresses a brother on my heart? Can I make the first move?

It is not out of place to receive the conviction about your spouse from God first. All you need to do is to prayerfully meet your pastor, a trusted elderly couple or a godly counselor to bare your mind to them. Do not do anything special to arouse the interest of the man towards you. Do not be in haste and control your emotions. After consulting with any of the above suggested people and they prayed with you and received a go-ahead from God, the man would be prayerfully met and discussed with. If he is already engaged, keep praying and do not be discouraged; your own spouse will come, and it may turn out to be the same person. Give room for refusal and do not give up so easily when you are your very sure.

The Lord shows us how we should live, and he is pleased when he sees people living that way. If they stumble, they will not fall, because the Lord reaches out to steady them. (Psalm 37:23-24)

6. Forgiveness is enjoined in the Bible; to what extent is it practicable in marriage?

Forgiveness is having compassion on the person who has done something wrong to you and putting the past behind you. That is, to receive the grace to forgive and forget the issue as if it never happened.

Firstly, the act of forgiving each other or one another, as the case may be, should be an attribute of every child of God. If God can forgive your countless sins, then you ought to forgive whoever offends you too.

Secondly, it is a commandment that must be obeyed and a prerequisite to your being blessed and to make heaven. In other words, if you refuse to forgive others, you cannot enter the kingdom of God. Marriage is an institution that is governed by God; forgiveness in marriage is therefore a therapy for healing in the home and for the body, soul and spirit.

Unforgiveness will hamper God's peace in your home. It will obstruct answers to your individual and joint prayers and may be used by the devil to penetrate into your home. It will engender strife, anger, malice and could lead to separation or divorce because it will become aggravated if not curbed on time. Every couple therefore, must cultivate the habit of not going to bed in anger, quarrel, malice or unforgiveness.

Don't be angry with each other, but forgive each other. If you feel someone has wronged you, forgive them. Forgive others because the Lord forgave you. (Colossians 3:13)

> If you dig a hole, you might fall into it. If you break down a wall, you might be bitten by a snake. (Ecclesiastes 10:8)

7. Can gifts be exchanged during courtship?

Yes, it can be exchanged but not without some precautions. The period of courtship and marriage is a time to share things with each other but it should not be the foundation of the union. You must ensure that the love between the two of you is not based on "material things" like houses, cars, money or other gifts. Search your heart and ask yourself this vital and sincere question. If the gifts stop flowing, will my love and friendliness towards him still be the same?

Gifts, money, beauty and other material things should not be the source of your love for each other. Let there be an unfeigned love; a love without dissimulation between both of you.

> Money blinds the eyes of wise people and changes what a good person will say. (Deuteronomy 16:19b)

> Whoever takes money to do wrong invites disaster. Refuse such gifts, and you will live. (Proverbs 15:27)

8. What harm will premarital sex do to our relationship since both of us is in love?

It is an act of disobedience towards God. Indulging in it will make you guilty; it will deny you of having the right access to God because it is a sinful act and God hates sin. The devil will use it against you; and you may go through some problems in your marriage as a result of it. Even if it does not lead to pregnancy, God will always castigate those who engage in such sins; sex should be practiced within marriage alone. If you are not married, you are not married.

> Don't you know that you are God's temple and that God's spirit lives in you? If anyone destroys God's temple, God will destroy him because God's temple is holy. You are that holy temple! (I Corinthians 3:16-17)

> Marriage is honourable in every way, so husbands and wives should be faithful to each other. God will judge those who commit sexual sins, especially those who commit adultery. (Hebrews 13:4)

9. Is it possible for anyone not to indulge in pre-marital sex?

It is possible. Having given your life to the Lord Jesus Christ, you will be given a new heart that is pure and holy. All you need to do is to abstain from all appearance of evil and ask for the grace to live above sin; because you cannot achieve this feat on your own. Every normal human being has strengths and weaknesses; you should identify your weak points and work on it. Desist from anything that will make you fall prey to the tactics of the devil, do not go to where you will be lured into sexual sin. Make sure your friends are the type that will help you avoid such limitations; avoid reading or watching anything that will stir you up sexually and, above all, be prayerful and meditate on the word of God. Moreover, if you are easily tempted to go into sexual sins, then go for counseling and deliverance.

Additionally, to narrow the answer down to your would-be spouse, avoid visiting him alone; always visit each other where there is a third party and engage in worthwhile activities whenever you are together. To my beautiful lady, do not expose your nakedness to your fiancé; remember that you are not married until you are married. If you have any reason to go out together and stop over at a friend's or a relative's home in the night, insist on sleeping in separate rooms, no matter how much they prevail on or cajole you into sleeping together.

> **Stay away from the evil things a young person like you typically wants to do. Do your best to live right and to have faith, love, and peace, together with others who trust in the Lord with pure hearts. (2 Timothy 2:22)**

> **Dear friends, you are like visitors and strangers in this world. So, I beg you to keep your lives free from the evil things you want to do, those desires that fight against your true selves. (I Peter 2:11)**

10. A lot of times I am scared of waiting long for my spouse because of the prophecy of seven women hanging on one man just to bear his name in the book of Isaiah 4:1.

Providence has ordered it that in an average number of years, there are nearly an equal number of males and females born into the world. As there are deaths attending the bringing forth of children which are peculiar to women, there are deaths common to men which are experienced during the war, communal clashes and other calamities; hence the prophecy of seven women to one man. However, at the end of a tunnel, there is a road; even though everything may look dim, the sun will always break out from the cloud. In Isaiah, chapter 4 verse 2, there are precious promises of assurance and comfort, which points us to the kingdom of the Messiah and the great redemption to be brought by him.

Through the Messiah, the gospel will be embraced; the branch of the Lord will stand out of the stem of Jesse and a branch out of His roots shall produce the fruit of the earth. As many that are saved are under a new and a better covenant. God will rectify whatever is faulty in their foundations; they will be called holy when the Lord would have washed away their sins with His blood. In other words, this problem would be removed from the lives of His children. God will protect them by defending their tabernacles. He will arise on their behalf to save them from the wind and thunderstorm. He will be their hiding place and refuge in the time of storm. Therefore, if you believe in miracles and that, when God speaks, He hastens to perform it, then He will not let you down, He will give you your own husband at the appointed time. He gave Eve to Adam, he would connect you to your own husband, in Jesus' name.

God can do anything. (Luke 1:37)

And if you ask for anything in my name, I will do it for you. Then the Father's glory will be shown through the Son. If you ask me for anything in my name, I will do it. (John 14:13:14)

You have come to Jesus – the one who brought the new agreement from God to his people. You have come to the sprinkled blood that tells us about better things than the blood of Abel. (Heb. 12:24)

11. What should I do if physical disability occurs to my partner during courtship?

I will strongly counsel you to continue with the relationship if you are sure of being led by God and if you truly love him. Naturally, the fear of the unknown of the future may set in, but you will pull through with God. Faith in God, determination and love for him are all you need and He will see you through.

> **Lord God, with your great power you made the earth and the sky. There is nothing too hard for you to do. (Jeremiah 32:27)**

> **The Lord watches over his followers, those who wait for him to show his faithful love. He saves them from death. He gives them strength when they are hungry. (Psalm 33:18-19)**

12. I am in a relationship and I discover that my partner has a perceived foundational problem; a curse was placed on his family by the gods of their land. What should I do?

In a relationship that is bound to endure, since you are convinced that you are led to each other by God, then you should not hide anything from each other: spiritual, physical or emotional. You should not spend your courtship period in deception; rather you must tell each other everything that you can remember about yourselves and your families.

Do not plays hide and seek with each other. Hence, if you have revealed this incident to your partner; then it is advisable you go for counseling and deliverance before you are joined together.

However, it may not necessarily stop you getting married to the person, unless you receive a message from the Lord to discontinue the relationship. Do the right thing first by going for deliverance and the two of you should also engage in intense prayers towards your union.

Knowing very well that the God you are serving is a great God is who is able to subdue all powers. The gods of the land would be subdued to rise no more, in Jesus' name. However, depart completely from sin. Do not live in fear because fear is the opposite of faith. Have strong faith in

God after praying and do not compromise your stand as a believer.

Peradventure you do not know before getting married, then get ready to "weather" the storm mutually in prayer, fasting and deliverance, not despising each other or regretting your decision to be together especially if you got married according to the will of God, He will definitely see you through. Since curses differ from one person to the other, seek godly counsel from the right minister of God who will teach you how to go about the restitution, if necessary, and undergo deliverance as you would be instructed. Make the necessary restitution and do not go back to your vomit.

> **All the "gods" in other nations are nothing but statues, but the Lord made the heavens. (I Chronicles 16:26)**
>
> **The gods of other nations are only gold and silver idols that the people have made. They have mouths, but cannot speak. They have mouths, but no breath. Those who make idols and trust in them will become just like the idols they have made. (Psalms 135:15-18)**

13. Should I continue with the relationship if we have conflicting genotypes?

This is a very serious issue that should be pursued with all sincerity. What applies to the individual whose spouse has a physical disability is also relevant to you but with a multiplying effect if you are not sure of what you are doing.

Firstly, you must be sure that the Lord has spoken to you concerning the issue in question and you must have accepted His will and He would give you the grace to do His will. Secondly, you must have enough faith to sail through the challenges that may come your way depending on your level of closeness to God. If you are not convinced of God's leading in the relationship and you do not have enough faith, then you had better drop the idea of getting married to the person.

If you are sure it is the Lord who has led you into the relationship, you can pray to God for His divine intervention and healing, He has done it before in the lives of others and yours will not be an exception.

However, medically, it is not advisable for anyone with conflicting genotypes like AS and AS to marry each other. They may have children with SS. Also, AS and SS should not think of marrying each other. They may not escape having children with the sickle cell disease. Kindly see your doctor for further counsel and medical advice.

> **Do any of you need wisdom? Ask God for it. He is generous and enjoys giving to everyone. So, he will give you wisdom. (James 1:5)**

> **Jesus answered, 'Have faith in God. The truth is, you can say to this mountain, 'Go mountain, fall into the sea.' And if you have no doubts in your mind and believe that what you say will happen, then God will do it for you. (Mark 11:22-23)**

14. Is childlessness avoidable? If it arises, how should a couple cope with it?

Our God is a God of possibilities and he still performs miracles. While we do not pray for childlessness in marriages, once in a while we have cases like this in marriages but we pray that it will not be anyone's portion, in Jesus' name.

You are encouraged not to live your youthful ages carelessly or waywardly. Avoid pre-marital sex that may lead to unwanted pregnancy and abortion, which may lead to evacuation of the womb in case of complications.

However, your salvation marks a difference between you and your past. Turn your life to the one who can make all things new for you, He will renew your life, in Jesus' name. The causes of childlessness could be spiritual or physical, but all these are under God's power.

During the period of waiting on God for your child and heritage, you can exert your energy on other things that will add value to your life physically and eternally rewarding, such as evangelism, skill acquisition, education, taking care of the less privileged children, widows and career development. By engaging in any of the above gainful activities, you would have added more feathers to your cap while waiting for your child.

Additionally, you will have more spiritual children before your own biological children will come. However, love towards each other, faith in God and living an uncompromising life will earn you earthly and heavenly rewards at the end of your race. Be conscious of the fact that childlessness must not hinder you from making heaven because genetic children are not the criteria for reigning with Christ.

You can pray about adopting a child while waiting for your child. Get the go-ahead from God before doing this. Ensure you follow the right procedure by using the legal means and from the appropriate and well-established orphanage homes.

Marrying a second or third husband or wife is neither a solution nor is divorce an answer to the problem. Do not add to the crisis by contravening God's laws.

Trust the Lord completely, and don't depend on your own knowledge. With every step you take, think about what he wants, and he will help you go the right way. (Proverbs 3:5-6)

Your women will all be able to have babies.

None of their babies will die at birth. And I will allow you to live long lives.

15. Why must I submit to my husband in marriage?

Submission is the act of accepting or yielding to a superior force or to the will or authority of another person. It is an act that is expressed mutually and voluntarily. Being submissive helps us to be less self-centered and allows us to consider the desires of others.

Submission has nothing to do with being weak, but allows us to be strong enough to open our hearts to others. Marital submission is when a wife voluntarily and willingly chooses to submit herself under her husband's leadership and authority. A wife is actually submitting to God by submitting to her husband. This is not to say that the woman cannot disagree with or express her opinion

The man should also submit to the woman's need to be loved. The woman's submission to her spouse is not because of his age, stature, position or influence. It is an obligatory injunction from the Lord that must be obeyed.

When you are submissive to him, he will also submit to you, but if you are arrogant, nagging and uncorrectable, these attitudes will upset him and it may lead to quarrel and lack of peace in the home. Pride and fear of submission are the enemies of submission. Submission will enable your husband have a sense of belonging and it will make him happy and loving towards you.

Wives, be willing to serve your husbands the same as Lord. A husband is the head of his wife, just as Christ is the head of the church. Christ is the Saviour of the church, which is his body. (Ephesians 5:22-23)

16. What would you advise about joint account?

A joint account is a bank account that is jointly owned and operated by a couple after mutual agreements between them. There are many ways to operate a joint account. The couple can operate an account where two of them will have specific amount that will be saved monthly or at an agreed time.

Where the wife is not working or engaged in any business, the husband must ensure that she does not lack anything according to God's provision for him. He must give her a specific amount for her daily upkeep.

You can also have a domestic or miscellaneous account where money meant for anything that may come up unexpectedly in the home is kept. This will be possible where both of you are earning money.

Additionally, the wife must be hardworking and have a means of earning money too so that she can contribute financially to the running of the home to avoid the financial burden being on the man alone. It is also advisable for the couple to save money for the rainy days. Putting 'all eggs in one basket' is not worthwhile.

Some of the advantages of joint account are teamwork, saving on children's fees, convenience, and equality even when the incomes are not equal; the couple contributes their fair share to the upkeep of the home. The drawbacks may be the need to take decisions on purchase anytime the need arises and individual purchase of gifts may not be easy.

> **Two people will not walk together unless they have agreed to do so. (Amos 3:3)**

> **In the same way, you husbands should live with your wives in an understanding way since they are weaker than you. You should show them respect, because God gives them the same blessings, he gives you –the grace of true life. Do this so that nothing will stop your prayers from being heard. (I Peter 3:7)**

17. How elaborate should a wedding be?

The expenses you will incur on your wedding is a function of the money you have planned to spend on the wedding ceremony. The Bible says, 'Let your moderation be known unto all men, the Lord is at hand.' You should be modest in your expenditure. Make a list of all the necessary things you need prior to the wedding and implement each of them in order of priority. Plan with what you have in your account or what you have set aside to spend on the occasion.

As much as possible, avoid borrowing or spending to satisfy the people around you. As a true child of God, be yourself and do not struggle to be like any other person or listen to ungodly counsel that will impair your home from its foundation.

Ladies are prone to excessive spending when it comes to ceremonies; hence, be considerate with your spouse in whatever you want to do. If you celebrate the wedding ceremony with ten cows, people will gather to consume it and there may not be any left over, remember the wedding of Cana in Galilee.

If all you can afford is a cow, then make do with what you have. For your information, everything in life is a style. Sister Clara may sow a three-quarter length of wedding gown because that was what she could afford. You may force yourself to do the same thing without knowing that she was merely trying to cut her coat according to her cloth.

Brother Yemi and Sister Zainab could receive their wedding gown and suit free of charge from a popular designer in the United Kingdom. You might wish to have the same dress immediately you set your eyes on the outfits without knowing the attires were given to them at no cost. Be moderate and be yourself at all times. Bear it in mind that the real home is still there. Do not start your marital life with people knocking on your door to ask for the money lent to you for your wedding ceremony; it can be demoralizing.

> **Let your moderation be known unto all men, The Lord is at hand. (Philippians 4:5 KJV)**

> **Everything you say and everything you do should be done for Jesus your Lord. And in all you do, give thanks to God, the Father through Jesus. (Colossians 3:17)**

18. Is it advisable to keep house-help in my home?

House-helps are "necessary evils." You may need to ask yourself the following questions before taking the decision to hire a house-help. Why do I need him or her? Can't I make an alternative arrangement for my home instead of engaging a stranger? What gender should I hire, especially with the high rate of sexual abuse on both sexes, but the girls are mostly affected? What about the spiritual implications? I do not expect newly married couples to engage the service of a house-help in their homes. Also, if you are not a working-class lady, you may not need one until you have one or two children.

We are all aware of the havocs these creatures have caused in homes. You can employ a laundry man or woman, while you perform the other house chores by yourself and with the help of your spouse. If you have to take one for health reasons or because of the nature of your job, then you will have to seek God's face for a go-ahead and for his favour in getting a good one. Engage your new house-help in warfare prayers, especially in the night.

Also, instead of allowing a total stranger to take over your home completely, you may employ the services of a house-help that would resume in the morning and close for work in the evening. If your kids are females, be wise enough not to employ a male house-help. Be vigilant; be very close to your children by asking them questions and do not leave your kids with neighbours that you cannot vouch for.

In addition, make sure you allow your children to participate in house chores as they grow up, failing which, you might be building another child's life at the expense of your own.

> **Teach the children in a way that fits their needs, and even when they are old, they will not leave the right path. (Proverbs 22:6)**

19. How involved must the children be in house chores?

The children must participate in house chores even when you have a house help. The Bible says, 'Teach the children in a way that fits their needs, and even when they are old, they will not leave the right path."

As soon as a child attains the age of six, he or she should start learning little household tasks like washing plates after eating and washing his or her pants. You have got to catch them young and on time too. Also, endeavour to lead by example. A lazy mother would breed lazy children. Every parent must be up and doing to teach the children to be of good behavior: the girls and the boys alike.

To the ladies, no matter your level of education, if you are not a good cook and a homemaker, you will not be respected in your home. You will turn out to be a bad mother and it will rub off on your parents because your inability to cook well could mean two things; either you were not taught or you were not ready to learn. Learn how to cook new recipes and make your home habitable.

To the men, learn how to do house chores and be a good cook as well. Occasionally, you may be required to help your wife whenever she is tired, pregnant or just delivered of a baby. You should leave a good legacy for the boys that the house chores are not meant for the women alone. However, let the ladies know that the men are just lending a helping hand; their assistance should not be taken for granted.

> **Be sure to teach them to your children. Talk about these commands when you sit in your house and when you walk on the road. Talk about them when you lie down and when you get up. (Deuteronomy 6:6)**

20. Is family planning important in a home?

According to the World Health Organization (WHO), family planning is defined as 'the ability of individuals and couples to anticipate and attain their desired number of children and the spacing and timing of their births. It helps to prevent unwanted pregnancies and undesired deaths of mothers and children.

I belong to the school of thought of those who believe in rearing godly seeds and not a set of unwanted and unplanned children. Spacing your children will also afford you the opportunity to raise the children properly. Investing into your kid's life spiritually, physically, emotionally and educationally is a venture that is really worth it. Hence, for you to raise godly children, you must give birth to the number of children that you can handle effectively. There are no second chances, because you will live with its consequences.

It is, therefore essential that you space your children and give birth to the number of children that you know the Lord will help you to raise and they will still be able to reverence God in their lives. Remember, you are only a caretaker of these offspring and their well-being in all aspect is very important and rewarding. Seek the advice of a medical professional before using any kind of family planning method.

Everyone should take care of their own

people. Most important, they should take care of their own family. If they do not do that, then they do not accept what we believe. They are worse than someone who does not even believe in God. (I Timothy 5:8)

21. How cordial must I be with my in-laws?

Your relationship with your in-laws must be warm and friendly. You must relate with them with love and without any misconception, knowing that you will be an in-law to someone in the nearest future, if Christ tarries.

As a true child of God, you must follow peace with all men and holiness, without which no man shall see the Lord. You are a letter written in the hearts of men, not written with ink, pen or tablet made of stone, and whatever you do in words or deed, do all in the name of the Lord.

Do not treat them with disdain; accept them as the extended members of your nuclear family. Be close to them and relate with them with wisdom. Be generous to them. Be a good example of Christ by allowing your life to witness to them that Jesus reigns in your home and that there is a difference between an unbelieving wife and a Christian woman.

Do not starve them whenever they visit you, neither should you borrow anything to satisfy them. Let them know when you have money and when you do not have. Avoid unannounced visits from them into your home any day on a wrong assumption that they will always get whatever they want whenever they visit you.

Additionally, do not join the band wagon of ungodly ladies who are praying that their mother-in-laws should die before they get married.

Although, we know that there are some bad in-laws, if you are still single, you can turn the tide around by praying that the Lord will lead you and your siblings to good in-laws and God will answer your prayers. If you are already married, you can still cry unto the Lord and he that made them will change them to the best.

> **Love each other in a way that makes you feel close like brothers and sisters. And give each other more honour than you give yourself. (Romans 12:10)**
>
> **Try to live in peace with everyone. And try to keep your lives free from sin. Anyone whose life is not holy will never see the Lord. (Hebrews 12:14)**

22. What do I engage myself with during the period of waiting for my spouse?

As it is with other periods of waiting on the Lord, you must be of good courage and God will strengthen your heart. The period of waiting for your spouse should be spent in the service of your Master. Do not allow the devil have an edge over you by whispering to you that you have come to your wit's end. Remember, it is not over until it is over; so, do not give up. Join the work force of your local assembly and serve in an identified department; it may be ushering, choir, Sunday school, Counseling, hospitality and so on. Do not be idle at all, the devil finds work for idle hands.

Appear graciously all the time by letting the glory of the Lord be seen in you as you dress modestly, decently and neatly to glorify God. If you are blessed financially, you can use the period to improve your spiritual and educational levels by going to school to further your education in addition to the secular work or business that you are doing. There are many online courses that you can take advantage of during the time of waiting.

The Bible says, **'The just shall live by faith.'** Therefore, let positive confessions be part of you. Do not sell yourself cheaply to the opposite sex by forcing yourself on them in the name of friendship.

Do not be a victim of guys who get so close to ladies without proposing to them. Ironically, they give these ladies the shock of their lives when the latter wait endlessly without the former asking for their hands in marriage; only to come up one day with a wedding invite.

The brothers who probably prayed and were convinced about these ladies would not want to express their desires to them because of the guys who were closer to them.

Don't be envious when the wedding invite of your friend is out. **'Rejoice with those who are rejoicing'** Your day of rejoicing will definitely come, in Jesus' name. Above all, be prayerful, have faith in God. Be sensitive in the spirit and do not be proud.

To further answer the question on 'what to do during the period of waiting', I'd like to refer to the message delivered by Mrs. Tosin Adefala during the Lady in Waiting program with the ladies in the Pearly Gates and 'Her' group.

The Right Way to Wait: Things to do while waiting.
Grow Spiritually:

Ensure that you have a personal relationship with God. This way, when he speaks concerning any area of your life, you will hear him clearly.

1. How can you grow in Him?
Use the GROWTH acronym.

G - Go to Him in prayers concerning all areas of your life.
    (Luke 18:1; I Thessalonians 5:17)

R - Read and meditate daily on His word.
    (Psalms 119:9, 11; Joshua 1:8)

O - Obey God's word. (I Samuel 15:22)

W - Witness the word (II Timothy 4:2)

T - Trust in God always. (Proverbs 3:5; Hebrews 11:1)

H –Holiness: Avoid sin, do not allow yourself to be

tempted. (Hebrews 12:14)

2. **Develop yourself**
   a. Know who you are.
   b. Know where you come from.
   c. Know where you are going.
3. **Do not put a strict timeline on marriage.**
4. **Shine your 'outer and inner' eyes.**
6. **Begin to live your best now** (John 10:10b)

Tosin Adefala concluded by saying, 'God loves you and He wants you to be sold out to Him, He wants you to know that He has great desires and plans for you that you must achieve whether married or not. Your single years are delicate and you must hold them as such; Guard your heart jealously, think and walk with your head high up, confident in the fact that you are God's own lady, walking in His will and purpose, basking in the abundant life that He has given you and very confident that He will bring your way that great man that He has planned for you.'

23a. When do I talk to my kids about sex?

The children should be taught sex education immediately they start talking and can identify who they are. You will start by teaching the child the names of the parts of the body. For instance, you should tell your child, 'This is your penis.' 'Instead of 'your pp.' Breasts should be called breasts and not 'oranges.' Let him or her also know that nobody should fondle with the private parts of their bodies. You can start to educate your kids from the age of two.

b. With the current rate of sexual abuse in the entire world, what can a parent do?

*Pray for your children relentlessly. Make conscious effort to ensure that they are saved and disciple them.

*Teach them the word of God continuously. This will help them to know the right to behave and who to make friends with when peer pressure sets in.

*Start teaching your wards sexuality education the moment they start talking and can identify the parts of their bodies.

*Teach them the real names of their private parts.

*Be available for your children. Do not substitute your presence with outrageous gifts and spontaneous outings to exciting places.

*Love and punish them when they err, but let them know why they're being punished. If you do not desire to spare the rod; if you want use cane to correct bad behaviours, don't make it a norm. Boys and girls treat the cane disdainfully these days. They stretch their hands to you before you cane them and shove off the pain with pride in your presence. Use cane irregularly for severe offences.

*Watch what they read and watch on television, computer and other social media.

*Have a zero tolerance for pornographic films or pictures in your homes and let them know that it is out rightly wrong to view it from anywhere.

*Do not expose your nakedness before your children. This goes to both parents. Fathers should stop wearing revealing boxers. Mothers should stop tying wrappers around the house, dressing up before your wards or having your baths with them. If you can afford it, separate the girls' and the boys' rooms. Teach them not to dress up before themselves.

*Be sure of where your kids spend the holidays. So many sexual abuses emanate from where the kids go for holiday - for boys and girls.

*Watch the people (family and friends - both genders) who live with you and visit you. When you go out to visit friends and families, be very vigilant about where and who your children mingle with.

*Teach them to dress well and not to expose their nakedness. Let them know the boundary between dressing well and dressing to seduce.

*Watch what you say to them and what you discuss with your spouse and visitors when they are around you. Teach them to excuse you when the adults are discussing.

*Make conscious effort to know how they're faring wherever they are: home, school, religious places, society etc.

*Be friendly with them. Give them the opportunity to trust and build confidence in you. This will help them to tell you deep things that may be haunting them.

*Create a good atmosphere between you and your children to make you the first person they discuss with whenever they have challenges, irrespective of their ages.

*Be involved prayerfully and proactively in the stages of their relationships. However, do not pressurize them into making hasty, wrong choices. Prayerful guide them regarding their marital thoughts, desires and plans.

*Help them not to have low self-esteem. This will help them to be bold and courageous wherever they are.

*Do not leave your children with neighbours or friends that you cannot vouch for.

> **Always remember these commands that I give you today. Be sure to teach them to your children. Talk about these commands when you sit in your house and when you walk on the road. Talk about them when you lie down and when you get up. Tie them on your hands and wear them on your foreheads to help you remember my teachings. (Deuteronomy 6:6-8)**

> **We don't enjoy discipline when we get it. It is painful. But later, after we have learned our lesson from it, we will enjoy the peace that comes from doing what is right. (Hebrews 12:11)**

24. Can I borrow a wedding gown?

Experience and revelations have shown that such actions are done ignorantly; but it sometimes attracts severe consequences. Wedding gowns or suits are hallowed apparels that play significant roles in your life when worn on the wedding day. Some people's lives are made or marred through the attires worn on this day.

Some are very desperate that even after explaining to them that there is a problem with the wedding gown or suit, they intend to borrow, they would still want to use the same dress. If you were unfortunate to wear the attire that was 'charmed' then you are very likely to go through the pains and sorrows that were inflicted on the owner.

However, because of this probable occurrence, wear whatever you can afford on your wedding day and on every other day. Do not start your home by engaging in warfare prayers of an unknown curse. You already have many things to pray for. Whatever you can afford is yours; it is godly and it is best for you.

> **Devotion to God is, in fact, a way for people to be very rich, but only if it makes them satisfied with what they have. When we came into the world, we brought nothing. And when we die, we can take nothing out. So, if we have food and clothes, we will be satisfied with that. (I Timothy 6:6-8)**

25. What in your own opinion are the secrets of a successful marriage?

Newly married couples are admonished to stay together if possible, during the initial years of their matrimony: to give the union a chance to mature and be fortified before they will meet head-on with numerous social responsibilities. A gardener starts a tiny seedling in a small pot and allows it to take root before planting it in the field. Let your marriage grow strong by guarding it from many outside influences, especially at the inception of the union.

In the same vein, you should avoid bringing into your home your extended family members from the onset. You are just getting to know each other and you need time and intimacy to achieve this. It could work for some people, but it may or may not go down well with your home. Therefore, pray earnestly over this issue before starting your marriage.

Furthermore, love plays a key role in the success of the home as clarified in **I Corinthians, chapter 13:4-7**

> **Love is patient and kind. Love is not jealous, it does not brag, and it is not proud. Love is not rude, it is not selfish, and it cannot be made angry easily. Love does not remember wrongs done against it. Love is never happy when others do wrong, but it is always happy with the truth. Love never gives up on people. It never stops treating, never loses hope, and never quits. Love will never end.**

The marriage venture, like every other business enterprise requires an uncompromising commitment. Both of you must be committed to its success; shedding off every impediment on the way to making your marriage a good example to all and sundry.

You must understand each other, despite your various ethnic, cultural, or social disparities. Both of you must prayerfully adjust to each other's differences. Discard the idea of third-party intervention in your home and do not compare your husband with another man. Let contentment rule your home; contentment is a choice that is made despite the temptation to be ruled by feelings.

Contentment is an action and a decision to be happy with what you have and it will bring a long-term bliss. In addition, your being contented does not mean that you will not pray about your present condition; but as you pray, let your subconscious mind not lust after what you are praying for.

Also, you must be tolerant; the ability to put up with

each other will neither make you stupid nor dense. It will only give room for adequate understanding of each other. You must not have the nagging nature, although, most men confuse women's persistent nature with nagging. God will help you to drive home your point accurately and settle the remaining on your knees instead of insisting on answers from your spouse all the time.

Do not deny your husband of his sexual right by giving flimsy excuses to substitute your unmet needs by him or declaring that you are tired when you are not. You will discover that apart from food, spiritual commitment, career and hobbies; one other crucial thing that men will not compromise and which can bring discord in the home is sexual union.

You must be a family that prays, studies the Bible and fellowship together. 'The family that prays together stays together.' When you pray and fellowship together, it will not allow you to harbour unforgiveness, which may hinder your prayers. Set apart a time to seek God's face in prayer and fasting as a family. Make God your source and not your husband. He is also looking up to God to provide for his needs.

Finally, take a look at some of the unavoidable virtues that will make you a woman that God wants you to be; a blessing to your family and generation.

A highly educated lady is commendable, but a dirty lady will not be a good wife material.

A seasoned and brilliant career lady that is carefree and careless in the home will not be a good mother to her children and an amiable wife to her husband.

A fashionable lady with a good sense of dressing with attractive colour combination; but cannot cook nutritious and sumptuous meal for herself and her family will be dangerous to the family.

A highly spiritual and tongue-speaking lady that is not prudent, diligent and wasteful will make her home go bankruptcy.

What you need to be a great woman is not only being Spirit-filled, prayerful, tongue-speaking, highly educated but a combination of the above factors.

ABOUT THE AUTHOR

Funmilola Olunifesi is an ordained pastor and marriage counsellor in the Redeemed Christian Church of God. She has been ministering to singles and married couples for over two decades.

As an author, she has written *Strength for the Journey of Life* and a children bible study series called *Devotional Comics for Children*. She is the administrator of Nifesi Schools and has written academic textbooks for children in elementary and primary classes.

Funmilola Olunifesi is married to Lawrence, a pastor and engineer. Together, they are blessed with three gracious children.

www.ingramcontent.com/pod-product-compliance
Lightning Source LLC
Chambersburg PA
CBHW060350050426
42449CB00011B/2901